A PALMISTRY GUIDEBOOK

AND

HAND-PRINTING KIT

Everything You Need to Read and Create a Print of the Hand

HELENE SAUCEDO

Illustrations by Bonnie Clas

Harper DESIGN

An Imprint of HarperCollins Publishers

"The Guest House" from *The Essential Rumi* by Jalal al-Din Rumi.
Translation © 1995 Coleman Barks. Reprinted by permission of
Coleman Barks.

HANDFUL OF STARS

HarperCollins books may be purchased for educational, business, or
sales promotional use. For information please e-mail the Special Markets
Department at SPsales@harpercollins.com.

First published in 2019 by
Harper Design
An Imprint of HarperCollins *Publishers*
195 Broadway
New York, NY 10007
Tel: (212) 207-7000
Fax: (855) 746-6023
harperdesign@harpercollins.com
www.hc.com

Distributed throughout the world by
HarperCollins *Publishers*
195 Broadway
New York, NY 10007

ISBN 978-0-06-289936-1
Library of Congress Control Number: 2018965713

Book design by Raphael Geroni

Decorative corner elements on front of box and book cover:
© Shutterstock/Robert Castillo. ◆ Box tray liner and
background pattern on pages 4, 7, 64: © Shutterstock/PK55.

Printed in China

First Printing, 2019

For Parker

Your dreams are in your hands.

CONTENTS

THE GUEST HOUSE

This being human is a guest house,
Every morning a new arrival.

A joy, a depression, a meanness,
some momentary awareness comes
as an unexpected visitor.

Welcome and entertain them all!
Even if they're a crowd of sorrows,
who violently sweep your house
empty of its furniture,
still, treat each guest honorably.
He may be clearing you out
for some new delight.

The dark thought, the shame, the malice,
meet them at the door laughing,
and invite them in.

Be grateful for whoever comes,
because each has been sent
as a guide from beyond.

—Jalal al-Din Rumi
"The Guest House," thirteenth century
Translation by Coleman Barks

INTRODUCTION

FOR MORE THAN TWO MILLENNIA, humans around the world have used palmistry to unlock a deeper understanding of ourselves and our destinies. Palm reading most likely originated in India between 4000 and 1000 BCE; it also has roots in China and the Middle East, specifically Egypt. The Greeks and Romans were fascinated by palmistry, using it to diagnose illnesses and to determine a person's character. Evidence of its use as a tool to determine life expectancy dates to 350 BCE. In Aristotle's *The History of Animals*, he writes, "The inner part of the hand is termed the 'palm,' and is fleshy and divided by joints or lines: in the case of long-lived people by one or two extending right across, in the case of the short-lived by two, not so extending."

As a practice, especially for divination, palmistry has met with controversy over the centuries. During his reign in the 1500s, King Henry VIII banned the practices of both palmistry and astrology, and as the ruler of both the church and state of England, declared them pagan superstitions. In Bologna, Italy, in the 1550s, it is said that Bartolomeo della Rocca, who published the first book to investigate chiromancy (the now outdated term for palmistry), used it to predict the death of Italian military leader Ermes Bentivoglio in battle. Bentivoglio had della Rocca assassinated for the prediction. It is said that Bentivoglio did die in battle—although there are

some who believe he died by drowning. While palmistry took a downturn in popularity during the sixteenth century due to its association with witchcraft and magic, it became a subject of intrigue again during the seventeenth-century French Renaissance, as scholars tried to justify the practice through rational and scientific study, only to lose public interest again.

It wasn't until the late Victorian era that palmistry was accepted on a popular level, due mainly to the founding of the Chirological Society of Great Britain in 1889 and the American Chirological Society in 1897. Irishman John William Warner (who changed his name to Louis Hamon and wrote under the pen name Cheiro) published two very popular books— *Cheiro's Language of the Hand* in 1894 and *Palmistry for All* in 1896. An American doctor named William Benham also wrote a landmark book on the subject, *The Laws of Scientific Hand Reading* (1900). At this time, Captain Casimir Stanislaus D'Arpentigny, considered the father of French chirology—reading the hands to assess a person's psychological state rather than for divination—became the first person to determine a system of hand-shape classifications.

Hamon, or Cheiro, was a palmist to society, working in London and the United States. Some of his renowned clientele included Mark Twain, Oscar Wilde, Thomas Edison, Sarah Bernhardt, and the Prince of Wales (later, Edward VII). Cheiro also educated white-collar Americans on the pragmatic uses of hand analysis. As he writes in *Palmistry for All*, "In looking over the records of my career I find that in the course of my visits to America I gave private lessons to the heads of two hundred and seventy business establishments in New York, one hundred and thirty-five in Boston, and three hundred and forty-two in Chicago."

In 1943 Dr. Harold Cummins, considered the father of "dermatoglyphics" (his term for fingerprints and the lines on our hand and feet), published *Finger Prints, Palms, and Soles*, a medical text which included extensive research on the embryonic development of those characteristics. He found that our hand markings develop in utero about five months before birth. He also discovered that our fingerprints never change over the course of our lives, but the lines on our dominant hand do. This has not been scientifically proven, yet if you compare a child's hand with an adult's, you'll see that the child's hand will exhibit only the four major lines (the heart line, head line, life line, and line of stability), while the adult's will most likely have many more defined lines, all relative to the character of its owner. Dr. Cummins even compared dermatoglyphic patterns to a topographical map. Based on the idea of a map imprinted on our hands, modern hand analyst Richard Unger formed LifePrints, a system of hand reading and fingerprint analysis that claims it can determine one's life purpose by classifying the type of fingerprint held on each fingertip—whorl, tent, tented arch, or loop—and entering them into a systematic formula.

Over the ages, there's been skepticism about palmistry's validity, mostly because there are many often conflicting interpretations of the hand's various lines and features. These contradictions as well as the lack of evidence for palmistry's predictions, have caused palmistry to be viewed as a pseudoscience by academics. Despite that, scientists have tried to determine the validity of palmistry as an indicator of numerous physical and psychological health conditions over the years. In a study at the Bronx Municipal Hospital Center conducted between 1973 and 1975, Dr. H. Dar discovered that 3 to 4 percent of children with Down syndrome as well as 4 percent of newborns exposed to methadone while in the womb had a singular transverse palmar crease on their hand. In palmistry, a single transverse palmar crease is thought to be a combination of the top two major lines on the hand—the heart and head lines—and it cuts across the entire width of the palm where the heart and head line normally sit.

Nonetheless, there is an undeniable neurological connection between human hands and the brain. Hands are an integral part of our nervous system; some 17,000 skin receptors and 100,000 nerves live in the hand. Scientists consider hands a tool of the mind because they are more connected by sensory neuropathways to our brain than other parts of the body, except for the mouth and genitalia.

As a practicing hand analyst, I have found that the art of palmistry is about making connections. Reading the hand opens us up to see ourselves, revisit unresolved issues of the past, take stock of the present, and see the potential of the future. The hand is not only a tool that helps us see ourselves, but a way for humans to literally connect. Holding the hand of a near stranger while I read their palm dissolves the social anxieties that go along with meeting someone new and discussing intimate stories together. In our overstimulated world, I can't think of a more satisfying form of self-reflection. I also can't think of a more rewarding journey than sharing a simple method of discovering the wonders that lie in our hands with you.

HOW TO USE THIS BOOK

Things do not change; we change.

—Henry David Thoreau, *Walden*, 1854

IN *HANDFUL OF STARS* YOU'LL FIND EVERYTHING YOU NEED TO build and document a reading of the hand. Included is a guidebook that offers a collection of easy, efficient techniques for the most essential elements of a reading, along with perforated worksheets bound in at the back, a nontoxic ink pad, roller, and gel pen. After making a handprint on one of the worksheets, the reading begins!

The book is structured so that you can build a reading in a step-by-step fashion. I highly recommend that you follow the order of the book, as it begins with simpler components and works its way to more complex ones. Working in a different order than suggested won't change the reading, but it may complicate your understanding of the big picture.

The hand analysis is divided into three consecutive parts:

✦ AN EXAMINATION OF THE THUMB AND THE FLEXIBILITY OF THE HAND reveals a great deal about your identity in terms of your will, sense of logic and decision-making abilities, and the type of lifestyle that is most compatible with the level of stability you need.

✦ A STUDY OF THE SHAPE OF THE HAND AND THE PADDING AND POSITIONING OF THE FINGERS defines dominant personality traits.

✦ A READING OF THE PALMAR LINES provides the most intimate insight into your life path, including pinpointing specific past or future life events. Each palmar line, except for the heart line, has a timeline that represents your life span. Reading these lines paints a portrait of your personality, and the life you've lived, piece by piece.

As you move through each step in the book, you will find instructions on how to annotate your readings on the worksheet.

READ THE DOMINANT HAND

PALM READERS REFER TO THE HANDS AS EITHER DOMINANT OR recessive. The hand you write with is considered the dominant hand. The dominant hand represents your current state of being and your future. The markings on the dominant hand change over the course of our lives, reflecting our experiences and the changes we undergo.

If you're ambidextrous, assume your right hand is dominant. If you were born left-handed, but taught to write with your right hand, your left hand is dominant. If your hand contains a single transverse palmar crease, as shown in the illustration on page 46, consider the opposite hand dominant when printing and reading.

The recessive hand represents the destiny to which you were born, telling the story of your life as if it has already been written. Over a lifetime, lines on the recessive hand don't change drastically unless a person experiences unexpected life-altering events. While this book focuses on reading the dominant hand, it also shows you how to read and interpret the two hands together: see "Reading the Hands Together," page 60.

HOW TO MAKE A
HANDPRINT

WHETHER FOR PRACTICALITY OR PLAY, PRINTING THE hand is part of the human experience. The oldest known cave paintings, red handprint stencils found in Cáceres, Spain, have been dated to older than 64,000 years. Today, while kids still make handprints with tempera paint and impress them in clay, modern forensics uses biometrics, the calculated measuring of physical characteristics, to identify persons of interest in investigations through fingerprint identification. There's something satisfying and intimate about creating tactile reflections of our own bodies, and there's a story to be told in the printed lines made by our palms.

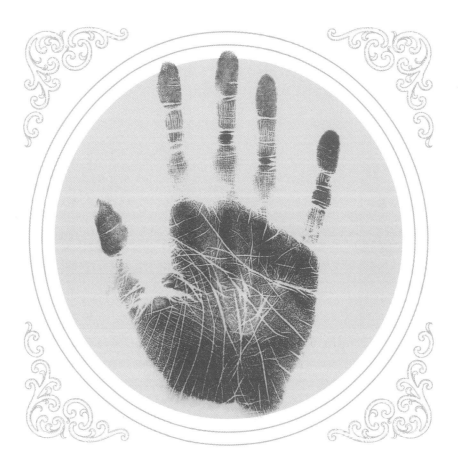

INSTRUCTIONS

FOLLOW THESE DIRECTIONS TO INK AND PRINT YOUR DOMINANT hand onto one of the worksheets at the back of the book. This print-making process involves using a medium-sized hand towel to capture a detailed handprint, so it's well worth taking the time to practice on plain paper until you get the hang of it.

YOU WILL NEED:

> Ink pad and roller (provided)
> Medium-sized hand towel
> A sink, with soap and water or wet wipes on hand
> Worksheet
> Plain paper, for practice
> Hair dryer (optional)

1. Tear out a perforated worksheet from the back of the book and place it on a clean, dry surface.

2. Move the roller back and forth on the pad until there is an even layer of ink on it. It is important that the ink transfer evenly from the roller onto your hand.

3. When inking the hand, start at the wrist and roll the ink toward the fingers. Be sure to roll the ink onto the hand in one direction: do not roll back and forth. Be sure to get ink on the thumb, the bottom of the fingers, and up inside the curve of the palm. Set the roller aside.

4. Sandwich the clean hand, palm facing upward, inside a folded towel. In terms of the quality of the impression, it doesn't matter whether the smooth or rough side is facing in or out.

5. Place the worksheet, right side up, on top of the toweled hand.

6. Bring the inked hand down on top of the worksheet and simultaneously push upward with the clean hand underneath, in order to get the print of the curve in the center of your palm. Make sure to capture the shape of the hand with the top parts of all your fingers, clear lines, and most of your thumb. Don't worry about attaining a completely perfect print; the bottom segments of the fingers are not important.

7. Set the worksheet aside on a clean surface. The print can be left to air-dry, although a hair dryer set on low and used gently may help it dry faster.

NAME Helene Saucedo **DATE** 10.31.19 **AGE** 39

HAND FLEXIBILITY standard

THUMB SIZE small

LOGIC VS. WILL logic > will

THUMB ANGLE intro

MOUNTS

♃ **JUPITER**
AMBITION · CONFIDENCE
A LEADER

♄ **SATURN**
DISCIPLINE · LIFE BALANCE
WORK ETHIC

☉ **APOLLO (SUN)**
CREATIVE · IMAGINATIVE
OPEN-MINDED

☿ **MERCURY**
COMMUNICATION · PROBLEM SOLVING
A SPEAKER

♀ **VENUS**
LOVE · BEAUTY
PLEASURE

☽ **LUNA (MOON)**
INTUITION · SPIRITUALITY
A DREAMER

♂ **MARS**
BRAVE · RESILIENT
A WARRIOR

ELEMENTAL SHAPE

▽ **EARTH**
PRACTICAL · GROUNDED
REALISTIC

△ **FIRE**
RESTLESS · ANXIOUS
WARM

△ **AIR**
INTELLECTUAL · CURIOUS
ADAPTABLE

▽ **WATER**
SENSITIVE · EMPATHIC
EMOTIONAL

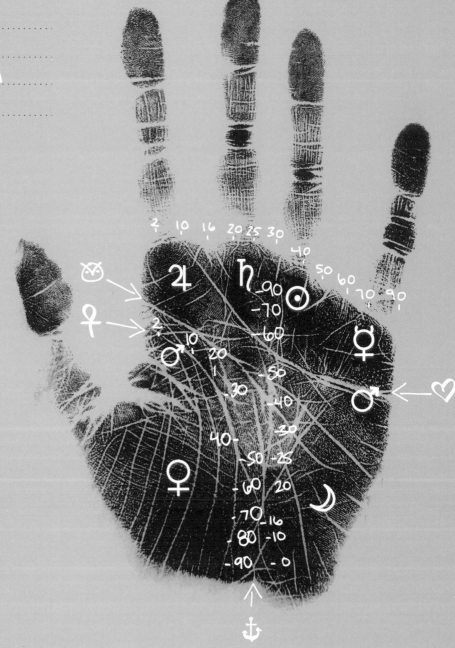

HOW TO FILL OUT THE WORKSHEET

ONCE YOU PRINT YOUR HAND ONTO THE WORKSHEET, YOU ARE ready to begin annotating the information you collect with the pen included in this kit. Each section of the book provides instructions on how to record your results as you work through the guided reading the text provides. Use the sample worksheet on the opposite page for reference.

Key Markings of the Hand: A Quick Guide

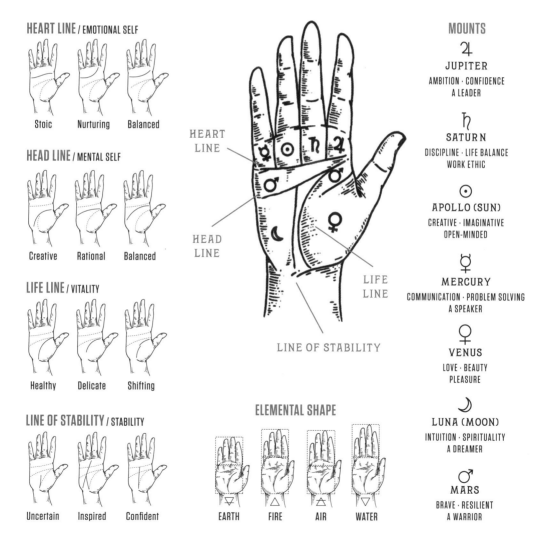

HEART LINE / EMOTIONAL SELF

Stoic · Nurturing · Balanced

HEAD LINE / MENTAL SELF

Creative · Rational · Balanced

LIFE LINE / VITALITY

Healthy · Delicate · Shifting

LINE OF STABILITY / STABILITY

Uncertain · Inspired · Confident

HEART LINE

HEAD LINE

LIFE LINE

LINE OF STABILITY

ELEMENTAL SHAPE

EARTH · FIRE · AIR · WATER

MOUNTS

♃
JUPITER
AMBITION · CONFIDENCE
A LEADER

♄
SATURN
DISCIPLINE · LIFE BALANCE
WORK ETHIC

☉
APOLLO (SUN)
CREATIVE · IMAGINATIVE
OPEN-MINDED

☿
MERCURY
COMMUNICATION · PROBLEM SOLVING
A SPEAKER

♀
VENUS
LOVE · BEAUTY
PLEASURE

☽
LUNA (MOON)
INTUITION · SPIRITUALITY
A DREAMER

♂
MARS
BRAVE · RESILIENT
A WARRIOR

HAND ANALYSIS

WHEN MOST PEOPLE THINK OF PALMISTRY, THEY IMAGINE IT AS the examination and interpretation of the four major lines of the palm: the heart line, head line, life line, and line of stability. These four lines can reveal a lot about a person's nature, but to get a more complete reading—one that reveals a thorough psychological picture—a palm reader examines the hand as a whole: the flexibility of the hand, the thumb and its various characteristics, and the overall shape of the hand. This is called hand analysis.

FLEXIBILITY

THE FLEXIBILITY OF THE HAND COMMUNICATES HOW MUCH structure you need to feel comfortable in day-to-day living, how you might handle sudden changes in your daily routine, from slight bumps on the road to greater disruptions. The more flexible the hand is, the more adaptable the personality.

How to Read

Sit down at a table, then straighten the arm of your dominant hand, palm facing upward, across it. Bend your elbow down so that it sits comfortably on the surface in front of you. Your entire arm and hand should look as if it were holding a serving tray.

Place your opposite hand on top of the fingers of the upward-facing hand, then gently push them down toward the table.

If the hand feels stiff, don't force it to move. Just note the level of flexibility.

How to Interpret

◆ **STIFF:** An inflexible hand indicates a person who thrives in a structured environment. Schedules, productivity, and routine are essential to their well-being. The unexpected is not particularly welcome. This is the hand of a person who truly needs to have things done their way.

◆ **SOMEWHAT FLEXIBLE:** A hand that stretches downward an inch or two represents a moderate level of adaptability and flexibility in career and relationships. This indicates a fairly adaptable personality, someone who can roll with the punches. In other words, change can be difficult, but this is a person who is willing and able to accommodate. Work/life balance is of the highest importance to those with somewhat flexible hands.

◆ **DOUBLE-JOINTED:** A double-jointed hand, one that pulls backward to 90 degrees, may not have much interest in following societal norms. An extremely flexible hand suggests an exceptionally open mind, abstract creativity, and an overall independent nature.

WORKSHEET

Fill in the result—stiff, somewhat flexible, or double-jointed—on the line labeled "hand flexibility."

THE THUMB

A goal without a plan is just a wish.

—Antoine de Saint-Exupéry, *The Little Prince*, 1943

READING THE THUMB IS A WAY TO DETERMINE BASIC PERSONALITY types (introvert vs. extrovert). It also helps us better understand a person's decision-making style (calculated vs. impulsive) and strength of determination. The thumb is read separately from the fingers because it moves in opposition to them, hence the term "opposable thumb."

THE SIZE OF THE THUMB

In palmistry, the thumb is categorized into three sizes—small, standard, and large. The size of the thumb is an indicator of a person's energy level as it applies to setting and working toward achieving goals. The thumb is also thought to reveal a person's priorities in terms of work/life balance, and whether they are a realist or dreamer.

How to Read

✦ Hold your dominant hand straight up with your fingers and thumb held tightly together. Make sure the thumb is pressed against the index finger. Note where the thumb hits on the bottom phalange (section) of the index finger; making a pen mark on the index finger where the top of the thumb ends can be helpful.

✦ A standard-sized thumb ends at the center of the bottom phalange. A large thumb measures higher than the center of the bottom phalange, while a small thumb measures lower than the center of the bottom phalange. If the measurement falls between these markers, round up or down according to visual approximation to the center.

How to Interpret

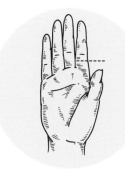

✦ **SMALL THUMB:** Those with small thumbs tend to take a keen interest in everyday beauty and nature. They have imaginative tendencies and prefer a looser life structure. Dreamers tend to have small thumbs.

✦ **STANDARD:** Balance is key for a person with a standard-sized thumb, especially when it comes to work and play. They seek equal parts productivity and downtime.

✦ **LARGE:** People with large thumbs are determined go-getters who don't take no for an answer. They're ambitious and energetic with high standards.

WORKSHEET

Write the size of your thumb on your worksheet in the blank next to "thumb size" with a short descriptor like "dreamer," "balanced," or "determined."

USING THE THUMB TO DETERMINE THE BALANCE OF LOGIC AND WILLPOWER

What one does is what counts and not
what one had the intention of doing.

—Pablo Picasso, "Picasso Speaks," *The Arts*, 1923

THE UPPER SECTION OF THE THUMB REPRESENTS LOGIC, WHILE the bottom portion represents willpower. Their relative proportion to each other is indicative of how they function together in decision-making processes.

How to Read

Hold the thumb of your dominant hand in front of you as if you are giving a thumbs-up. Note that it is divided into two sections, top and bottom, by a horizontal line near its center. Take note of each section's relative size to the other.

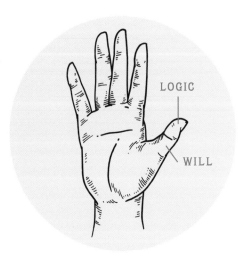

How to Interpret

✦ **LARGER TOP (LOGIC):** If the top section of the thumb is taller, this indicates a planner, a person who makes choices based on calculated measures. This person may tend to overthink or overanalyze a situation.

✦ **LARGER BOTTOM (WILL):** If the bottom portion of the thumb is taller than the top, this suggests a person who is not afraid to take risks. Their motto is act now, think later. Some might even say this person is impulsive.

✦ **TOP AND BOTTOM OF EQUAL PROPORTION:** If the two portions are equal in size, this signifies rationalized decision-making grounded in common sense. This is a person who weighs the pros and cons when making decisions and tends to take the appropriate action.

WORKSHEET

On the worksheet, label the top and bottom parts of the thumb handprint as "logic" and "will." When filling in the appropriate blank on the left side of the sheet, record your conclusion as:

✦ *"Logic > Will" (more logic than will)*
✦ *"Logic < Will" (logic less than will)*
✦ *"Logic = Will" (logic equal to will)*

THUMB AND PERSONALITY TYPE

THE ANGLE AT WHICH A PERSON HOLDS HER THUMB INDICATES an inclination toward introversion or extroversion.

How to Read

+ Shake your hand out gently for a few seconds to relax it.

+ Once the hand feels relaxed, abruptly stop shaking it and hold it up so that it is straight and still, but not stiff. If you overextended your fingers, shake your hand out and try again. The hand should feel comfortable as if you are naturally waving hello to a friend rather than preparing for a high five.

+ Take note of the open space created between the index finger and the thumb. The angle created between the two fingers acts as a barometer of personality type (introversion vs. extroversion). Refer to the diagram on the opposite page to find the measurement of the angle.

How to Interpret

+ **20 DEGREES OR LESS:** Introvert. Naturally quiet, withdrawn, and introspective, and most comfortable spending time alone. Nesting is important.

+ **20 TO 45 DEGREES:** An open introvert. Possesses the quiet qualities of an introvert but more comfortable in public than the introvert. This may indicate an introvert who's grown more comfortable in public; it can also indicate a person who requires and enjoys social connection, but recharging is essential.

+ **45 DEGREES:** Ambivert; equal parts introvert and extrovert.

+ **50 TO 80 DEGREES:** Extrovert. A person who is excited to engage with others and is at ease in groups.

+ **90 DEGREES:** Extreme extrovert. Thrives in social settings and may even feel uncomfortable when alone.

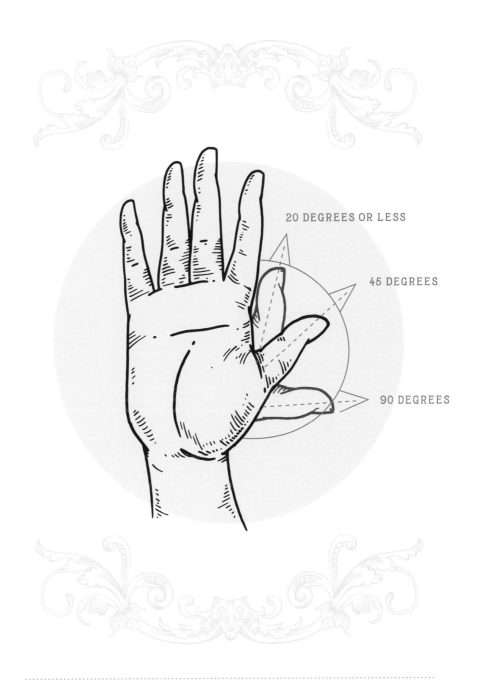

20 DEGREES OR LESS

45 DEGREES

90 DEGREES

WORKSHEET

Write down the angle at which you hold your thumb on the worksheet next to "thumb angle," as well as the personality type this angle suggests.

THE ELEMENTAL SHAPE
OF THE HAND

IN PALMISTRY, THE SHAPE OF THE HAND, SPECIFICALLY THE FORM of the palm and the proportion of our fingers to it, represents one of the four elements of nature: earth, fire, air, and water. Each element corresponds to a general personality type.

How to Read

The shape of the hand is determined by looking at the palm and fingers separately.

- ✦ PALM: Take note whether the palm is rectangular or square. Rectangular palms are longer than square-shaped palms, which appear to be even in length on all sides.

- ✦ FINGERS: Determine if the fingers are long or short, even if they appear to be a "normal" length. To do this, compare the length of your middle finger with the length of your palm: Hold your hand in front of you, with the palm facing toward you. Place a wooden pencil in front of the middle finger so that the eraser end sits at the base of that finger. With a Sharpie, draw a line on the pencil to mark where the top of your finger hits the wood. Measuring from the base of your fingers, compare that marked-off pencil length to the length of your palm. If the bottom of the pencil doesn't reach the bottom of the palm, you have "short" fingers. If the bottom of the pencil hits the top of your wrist or goes lower, you have long fingers.

The Zodiac and Hand Shape

The shape of the hand, like the twelve signs of the zodiac, can be categorized elementally as earth, fire, air, or water. Very often, a person's hand shape and zodiac sign fall under the same element: for example, a person who is a Cancer, a water sign, will have a water-shaped hand.

EARTH SIGNS: Taurus, Virgo, Capricorn
FIRE SIGNS: Aries, Leo, Sagittarius
AIR SIGNS: Aquarius, Gemini, Libra
WATER SIGNS: Cancer, Scorpio, Pisces

How to Interpret

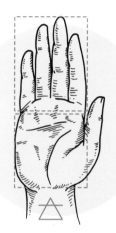

+ **EARTH HAND:** A square palm with short fingers. Earth hands are grounded, act with intent, and commonly possess only the major lines. Earth hands are the least sensitive of the four elements.

+ **AIR HAND:** A square palm with long fingers. The lines on air hands are typically light and thin, and there are few of them. People with air hands are adaptable, intellectual, and sensitive to the world around them.

+ **FIRE HAND:** A rectangular palm with short fingers. Fire hands often have many deep lines suggesting restlessness or anxiousness.

+ **WATER HAND:** A rectangular palm with long fingers. A water hand demonstrates sensitivity and intuition through many light lines. Empathetic individuals commonly have water hands.

WORKSHEET

Circle the element your hand represents from the list on the worksheet.

THE MOUNTS

MOUNTS, SHORT FOR MOUNTAINS, ARE THE FLESHY PADS
situated just below the fingers. There are eight mounts, and they encircle the palm. Each
mount represents our key personality traits derived from the characteristics exemplified
by gods from Greek and Roman mythology: Jupiter, Saturn, Apollo, Mercury, Venus,
Luna, and Mars (located in two places on the palm). They may be high and firm, high
and spongy, low, and in some cases, missing.

It is also common for more than one mount to be dominant. When this is the case,
the attributes of those mounts meld to further describe a distinctive character. Refer to
the chart on page 32 for assistance in interpreting their combined significance.

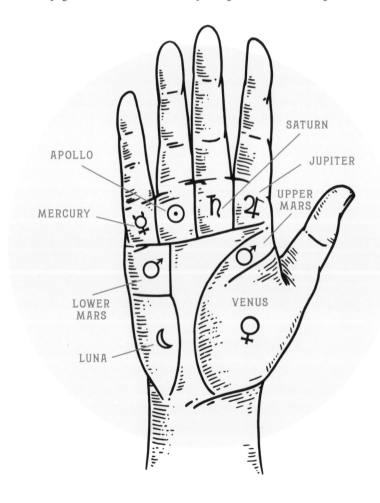

THE MOUNT OF JUPITER

The mount of Jupiter is located underneath the index finger. Jupiter, known as Zeus to the Greeks, was the king of the gods. Also called the God of Heavens, he overthrew his father, Saturn, to claim his throne. If the Jupiter mount is dominant, it indicates someone who is ambitious, goal-oriented, and enjoys the feeling of achievement. A well-developed mount of Jupiter suggests a confident, charismatic person, a leader, one who can guide and motivate others. However, if this mount is disproportionately larger than the rest of the mounts, this person should be aware of the fine line existing between confidence and arrogance that accompanies the driving force to succeed.

+ **HIGH AND FIRM:** Assertive, magnetic, a fearless leader.

+ **HIGH AND SPONGY:** Confident, ambitious, trustworthy.

+ **LOW:** Levelheaded leader, a role model, a guide.

+ **MISSING:** Apathetic, lacking in confidence and ambition.

THE MOUNT OF SATURN

Saturn, known as Cronus to the Greeks, overthrew his father, Uranus, the creator of the universe. The time of Saturn's rule is referred to as the Golden Age because of the peaceful way in which he ruled his nations; in keeping with that, the mount of Saturn represents life balance, discipline, and work ethic. Saturn is located underneath the middle finger. A person with a dominant mount of Saturn leads a balanced life in terms of responsibilities versus play, but when this mount dominates the hand to the extreme, there lies the risk of workaholism.

+ **HIGH AND FIRM, OR HIGH AND SPONGY:** Rare, but when seen it suggests the same characteristics as conveyed by "Low but wide compared with other mounts."

+ **LOW BUT WIDE COMPARED WITH OTHER MOUNTS:** Accountable, responsible, dependable.

+ **LOW AND NARROW COMPARED WITH OTHER MOUNTS:** Spontaneous, flighty, scattered.

THE MOUNT OF APOLLO

Apollo, the Greek and Roman god of the sun, music, poetry, and medicine, was also the leader of the Muses. The mount of Apollo is located underneath the ring finger. If this is the most pronounced mount, it suggests innate creative strengths. Often people equate creativity with artistry, but in the case of this mount, creativity refers to whatever opens the door to the imagination, however you apply it.

+ **HIGH AND FIRM (APPEARS AS TWO SMALLER MOUNTS SPLIT DOWN THE CENTER):** Innovative, visionary, unconventional thinker.

+ **HIGH AND SPONGY (APPEARS AS TWO SMALLER MOUNTS SPLIT DOWN THE CENTER):** Clever, inventive, creative-minded.

+ **LOW:** Open-minded, inspired, flexible, resourceful.

+ **MISSING:** Practical, pragmatic, realistic.

THE MOUNT OF MERCURY

Mercury, known as Hermes to the Greeks, is the Roman messenger to the gods and the god of business and games. The mount of Mercury is located underneath the little finger. A pronounced mount of Mercury belongs to a person who is skilled at communication, shrewd in business, or an adept problem solver. On a person with strong ideals or beliefs, be they religious, political, ethical, or social, the mount of Mercury will be developed. If this mount dominates the other mounts in an exaggerated way, this may indicate one who talks when they should be listening, or whose clever nature borderlines on trickster.

+ **HIGH AND FIRM:** A strong speaker, one who is persuasive or analytical.

+ **HIGH AND SPONGY:** Loquacious, long-winded, analytical, shrewd.

+ **LOW:** Expressive but calm in terms of verbal delivery.

+ **MISSING:** Secretive, guarded, and cautious.

THE MOUNT OF VENUS

Venus, called Aphrodite by the Greeks, is the Roman goddess of love and beauty. This mount is located on the inside of the thumb and occupies the bottom outer portion of the palm. This mount stands for more than romantic love; it embodies the joy of life's pleasures, such as arts and culture, food, beauty and sensuality. A person with a rounded mount of Venus is kind and open to new experiences. However, an excessively rounded mount of Venus may point to overindulgence or one who lives selfishly for pleasure.

+ HIGH AND FIRM: One who likes to travel and experience life, a romantic.

+ HIGH AND SPONGY: Self-indulgent, a pleasure seeker.

+ LOW: Warm, sympathetic, sophisticated, refined.

+ MISSING: Apathetic, rigid, prudish.

THE MOUNT OF LUNA

Luna, or Selene in Greek mythology, is the Roman goddess of the moon. The mount of Luna is located on the bottom half of the palm underneath the little finger. A person with a developed mount of Luna has access to inner realms of the subconscious, the magic of intuition, dreams, and mysticism. Luna and Venus are the most emotive mounts. Those people whose dominant hand displays more weight at the bottom, where these mounts lie, are capable of great feeling and arousing emotions in others.

+ HIGH AND FIRM: Spiritual, philosophical, even profound.

+ HIGH AND SPONGY: Intuitive, a dreamer, has an active interest in the metaphysical.

+ LOW: Sensitive, empathetic, imaginative.

+ MISSING: Skeptical, realistic, grounded.

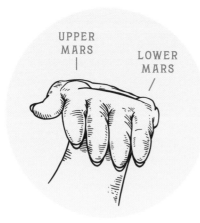

UPPER
MARS

LOWER
MARS

THE MOUNT OF MARS

Mars, Ares to the Greeks, is the Roman god of war. On the hand, the mount of Mars represents resilience and strength—one who has overcome significant obstacles in life. Mars is the only mount that exists on two distinct parts of the palm. Upper Mars is located on the little finger side of the hand, between the mount of Mercury and the mount of Luna; it represents the positive traits of a warrior: bravery and perseverance. Lower Mars is located horizontally across the palm from Upper Mars, underneath the index finger, between the mount of Jupiter and the mount of Venus, just above where the thumb attaches to the hand. Lower Mars represents confrontation and competitiveness—the more aggressive aspects of a warrior.

✦ **HIGH AND FIRM:** Resilient, brave, a fighter.

✦ **HIGH AND SPONGY:** Courageous or tenacious.

✦ **LOW:** Strong, persistent, and persevering.

✦ **MISSING:** Fragile, may be vulnerable or naïve.

HOW TO DETERMINE DOMINANT CHARACTER TRAITS

THE FIRST STEP IN ANALYZING THE MOUNTS IS TO COMPARE their heights. This will help us determine which traits are innate gifts, such as a natural ability to draw or an aptitude for finance. The second step is to look at the fingers as extensions of the mounts to discover which of these traits are being used at present and which are dormant. Perhaps we'll see there's an indication of great native creativity—and we may also see it's being utilized or experiencing serious blocks. The results are not to be interpreted as either good or bad. They just are what they are.

STEP ONE: EXAMINE THE HEIGHT OF THE MOUNTS

Some hands will have more pronounced mounts than others and are naturally easier to read. Don't let that discourage you. There is information to be gained by taking a close look. Take note of the most dominant mount and whether it obstructs other mounts. You may have just one dominant mount vying for attention, or all your mounts may appear fairly similar in height.

How to Read

+ Label your handprint with the symbols of the mounts shown in the diagram on page 26.

+ To judge the height of the mounts, hold your dominant hand out in front of you with your palm facing up.

+ Bring your palm up to eye level to compare the mounts, as follows:

  1. Observe the mount of Venus, next to the thumb. If it blocks the view of the mounts underneath the other fingers, this is most likely a dominant mount.

  2. Next, look to the mount of Luna, across from Venus on the opposite side of the hand. Luna can be a difficult mount to judge in terms of height, but if you push down onto the mount with one finger and there is a significant amount of bounce back, you can safely assume its qualities exist within you.

  3. The Jupiter mount is usually easy to spot and will stand fuller and taller than the rest of the mounts when dominant.

  4. The mount of Saturn is also known as the flat mount. Rather than being judged by its height, it is evaluated by comparing its width with the widths of the other mounts. This can be hard to determine by an untrained eye. Therefore, its presence is judged best by looking at the length of the middle finger. If the middle finger is noticeably longer than the other fingers, this is a sure sign Saturn is dominant.

  5. The mount of Apollo is split in two, resembling two small mountain peaks underneath the fourth finger. The two peaks can be hard to judge if they are not fleshy, so the mount may appear flat under the fourth finger with two taller pieces on either side.

  6. The mount of Mercury is easy to find. If it's dominant, it will stand tall under the little finger.

. . . .

WORKSHEET

Referring to the diagram on page 26, circle the corresponding mount(s) of the dominant trait(s) on the list on your worksheet. Depending on what you observe, it is possible to circle just one mount, multiple mounts, or all of the mounts.

MOUNT COMBINATIONS

IF YOU DISCOVERED THAT YOU HAVE TWO DOMINANT MOUNTS, refer to this chart, which highlights iconic individuals who, to my mind, encapsulate the personality of someone who possesses two mounts in these distinct combinations.

These selections do not suggest these individuals possess these mounts. I've used their names to suggest a certain energy they express.

Locate one mount on the top bar and the other mount on the side bar of the chart. Move your finger down from the top bar and across from the side bar: the point at which the chart converges points to the resulting combination.

We know what we are,
but not what we may be.

—William Shakespeare, *Hamlet*, 1603

	Jupiter	Saturn	Apollo	Mercury	Mars	Venus
Saturn	**NELSON MANDELA** Philanthropist or politician dedicated to bettering the interests of those he represents					
Apollo	**MICK JAGGER** Confident, creative showman	**THOMAS EDISON** Hardworking and pioneering in his chosen field				
Mercury	**BARACK OBAMA** Magnetic, a persuasive speaker	**AL GORE** Devoted to a singular cause and to educating others about it through different media	**WALT DISNEY** Highly imaginative, skilled communicator, and shrewd in business			
Mars	**RUTH BADER GINSBURG** Confident, a staunch defender of justice	**MARTIN LUTHER KING JR.** Pragmatic; makes his life work about effecting a focused humanitarian change	**PATTI SMITH** Champions the necessity of the freedom of personal expression	**BETTY FORD** A resilient warrior, one who has survived difficulties and shares her experiences to educate others		
Venus	**MAHATMA GANDHI** One who leads with compassion	**ANTHONY BOURDAIN** One who makes a career of his personal passions through hard work	**KEITH HARING** Artistic, one who conveys love for humanity through his work	**MADONNA** Advocate of open sexuality	**ANGELINA JOLIE** A dedicated humanitarian	
Luna	**DALAI LAMA** A born spiritual leader	**DEEPAK CHOPRA** Devoted to educating and advising others on spiritual matters	**C. S. LEWIS** Has strong mystical and spiritual beliefs and a desire to express them in an artistic form	**OPRAH WINFREY** Skilled in communicating spiritual and related beliefs effectively	**DESMOND TUTU** Deeply passionate about his spiritual or religious beliefs	**MOTHER TERESA** Highly intuitive, spiritually evolved, innately fueled by altruistic love

While viewing the height of the mounts reveals natural strengths, looking at the fingers reveals how those abilities are being used in the present. The fingers are considered extensions of the mounts that lie at their base, so only four mounts and fingers come into play in this exercise: the index finger (Jupiter), the middle finger (Saturn), the ring finger (Apollo), and the little finger (Mercury).

How to Read

+ Shake out your dominant hand for a few seconds to relax it. Once the hand feels relaxed, abruptly stop shaking and hold it up straight and still but not stiff. If you overextended your fingers, shake it out and try again. The hand should feel comfortable as if you are naturally waving hello to a friend rather than preparing for a high five.

+ It is helpful to imagine the four fingers are antennae that stem from the mounts at their base. Antennae are most receptive when straight and surrounded by space. A finger held in this way should be viewed as active.

+ Observe your index (Jupiter), middle (Saturn), ring (Apollo), and little (Mercury) fingers. Take note of which fingers are held straight, which are bent, and which are leaning on one another.

> **INACTIVE TRAITS** do not indicate downfalls or areas to improve. If a finger is inactive, it means its energy is not being tapped into at this moment.

How to Interpret

+ **INDEX FINGER:** An index finger that is held straight with space between it and the middle finger indicates a person who is actively confident, ambitious, or focused on achieving goals. Consequently, if Jupiter is bent, this may signify a person who is taking time off to enjoy life or perhaps is coasting at work. It is typical for a retired person or a young person taking a break before entering college to have a bent Jupiter finger.

✦ **MIDDLE FINGER:** If the middle finger is held straight, this indicates a person in work mode. This could be a busy time at work, exam time at school—whatever the task at hand, this person is busy and focused. If this finger is bent, this person is not interested in putting their nose to the grindstone at present. If this finger leans toward the Jupiter finger, it suggests hard work and ambition working together, with serious determination and effort being applied toward achieving a clear objective.

✦ **RING FINGER:** The Apollo finger is an open channel of creativity. A bent Apollo finger, or one that is leaning toward the Saturn finger, suggests blockage or ignored creative gifts. A graphic designer, artist, or writer more focused on logistics of business rather than the creative aspect of her work may also have this formation. This formation is not uncommon with a person who put down an instrument years ago because they simply didn't have the space in their life to practice or play.

✦ **LITTLE FINGER:** A straight little finger points to one who is presently using their communication or problem-solving skills effectively. If the Mercury finger is bent, this person may be keeping a secret or experiencing issues of discernment, struggling to find the right time at which to communicate information. Bent Mercury/little fingers can run in families as a form of a secret moving through generations. If you have a well-developed Mercury mount at the base of your little finger, but your little finger is naturally bent, look to see if either of your parents has a bent finger. It might not be that your personal communication skills are blocked, but that there is a family secret in your lineage.

WORKSHEET

Draw a star next to the corresponding mount(s) of your active trait(s) from the list on your worksheet.

MOUNT MARKINGS

AS A RULE, THE MORE SENSITIVE A PERSON IS, THE MORE LINES and markings are etched on the palm. Depending on the hand, mounts may have various marks on them, too. Read the brief descriptions below to reflect on what experiences your markings might symbolize in the context of the life area and qualities each mount represents.

Positive Marks

- **VERTICAL LINE:** Vertical lines represent positive experiences and strong skills related to the mount on which they live. A strong line on the mount of Jupiter, for example, illustrates an achievement in leadership.

- **TRIANGLE, SQUARE:** A triangle or square shields struggle, always protecting the mount where it lives. Either of these marks indicates there may have been trials in this area of life, but that they were ultimately overcome. A triangle on the mount of Saturn implies one who has had difficulty in creating a balanced life or has struggled to find motivation in terms of work but has overcome these issues.

- **TRIDENT:** A trident is the composite of multiple vertical lines that come to a head at their base. This is a mark of tenacious gifts in this life area.

- **STAR:** A star points to brilliance in this life area. A star on the mount of Apollo marks a creative genius.

Negative Marks

- **CROSSBAR OR X:** These symbols suggest complications, impediments, minor trials, or setbacks. An X on the mount of Mercury suggests difficulties in communication or the failure to express oneself clearly.

- **GRILLE:** A grille suggests difficulty or a blockage of the qualities of the mount. A grille on the mount of Luna may occur on the hand of someone who does not trust their intuition.

THE FOUR MAJOR LINES OF THE HAND

ATTEMPTING TO DECODE THE MYRIAD LINES IN THE PALM IS A deep dive into classical palm reading, one that's capable of overwhelming the amateur and professional alike. Fortunately, there are four major lines on the hand, and examining them one at a time, from different perspectives, is sufficient to craft a clear reading.

Think of the lines of the hand as rivers. Each of the four major lines represents a flow of energy coursing through the primary areas of the self. The heart line represents the emotional self; the head line, the mental self; the life line, vitality (contrary to myth, it is not an indicator of how long a person will live); the line of stability, stability. We'll also explore the single transverse palmar crease, which, although rare, is a fusion of the heart and head lines, and an indicator of a person who tends toward having great passions and drive.

A river flowing at its ideal potential is deep, long, straight, and without loss of force, and the same is true for the lines on the palm. If a line is deeper or longer than the others, it indicates that this life area is a driving force. A person whose heart line is deeper than the head line or life line, for example, will be guided through life more by feeling than by rational thought.

When reading each line, we'll first observe its overall appearance to establish an overarching perspective. Then we'll look more closely at the character of the line, which is revealed through distinct markings. Finally, we'll look at each line's timeline, which is useful for tracking events and changes throughout one's life. The heart line, head line, life line, and line of stability all have built-in timelines. Timelines are set according to our perception of time passing, which is why the beginning of life occupies a longer length of a line than the end of life does, with the last twenty years appearing as a much shorter section than other periods of life. Depending on the line itself, timelines span one's lifetime in various directions across the hand.

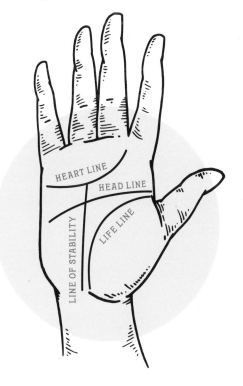

LINE MARKINGS

ALL LINES ON THE PALM MAY HOLD MARKINGS INDICATING specific events or actions. Hands with many markings may indicate a higher level of sensitivity or obstacles on a life journey.

The marks fall into three categories: positive (elations), negative (challenges), and neutral (both). Refer to the timelines for each line to track the age an event occurred in order to determine what a specific marking represents.

Before we look at the entries on the major lines, which each offer specific notes on distinctive markings and timelines, here's a list of the most common line markings and their significance.

Positive Line Markings

+ **TRIANGLE, SQUARE:** Protection. Resilience. A triangle or square implies triumph over hardship related to the line on which it lives.

+ **FORK, TRIDENT:** Calling-in of potential. Openness to receive. A fork or trident acts as a magnet that actively attracts experiences related to the line on which it lives.

+ **WELL-FORMED STAR:** Brilliance. Uniqueness. Stars are uncommon marks of illumination that indicate talent and marked individuality in the life area of the line.

Negative Line Markings

+ **CROSSBAR, X:** These suggest obstacles to varying degrees: a crossbar suggests minor difficulty; an X, a larger problem that has been faced.

+ **SPLIT:** Splits can be found on any line on the hand and mark overall shift, transformation, or loss, but on a smaller scale than a line break.

+ **LINE BREAK:** Line breaks mark moments when you feel you've lost control, or a major life event imposing change. If the line continues afterward, as it usually does, we see resilience.

+ **ISLAND, CHAIN:** Islands are metaphorical rocks in the rivers of energy of our lines. They represent problems we need to face. Repeating islands, called chains due to their likeness, suggest recurring complications or anxiety.

Neutral Line Markings

 ✦ **DOT**: A dot signifies a specific event. Dots are rare, and there are never many on any one hand.

 ✦ **TASSEL**: Tassels indicate confusion and uncertainty and are most often seen at the end of any of the major lines.

Have patience with everything
that remains unsolved in your heart...
live in the question.

—Rainer Maria Rilke, from *Letters to a Young Poet*, 1934

THE HEART LINE

THE HEART LINE IS THE TOPMOST LINE ON THE PALM AND explores the complicated nature of emotions. Examining the heart line is like lifting the veil of an individual's emotional life. The heart line is not all about romantic love: family, friendships, and work relationships live on this line, too. The heart line characteristically carries a higher number of islands than the rest of the major lines because we carry our emotions with us in everything we do. A dark heart line shaped by numerous interwoven lines exemplifies an intense emotional struggle, since the lines, or "rivers," look tumultuous.

When reading the heart line, look at its overall shape, depth, and length. The more curved the heart line is, the more accommodating a person can be for the sake of others. The straighter the line, the more stoic and independent a person's nature.

Look for markings at the beginning and at the end of the line to piece together a descriptive narrative of one's emotional life.

OVERALL SHAPE OF THE LINE: APPROACH TO LOVE, RELATIONSHIPS, AND EMOTIONS IN GENERAL

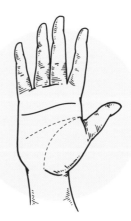

✦ **STRAIGHT AND SHORT:** This line indicates a person who is rational and composed or who may be inexpressive or inhibited. This heart line belongs to a person who may not be in touch with their emotions by nature, and that's not a problem for them.

✦ **STRAIGHT AND LONG:** This suggests someone who logically works through emotions. They tend to put themselves first and are cautious when forming new relationships and expressing feelings. This is a person of pride and integrity who enjoys their independence.

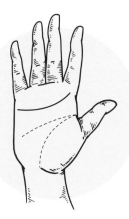

+ **CURVED UPWARD TOWARD, BUT NOT REACHING, THE TOP OF THE PALM, BETWEEN THE JUPITER AND SATURN FINGER:** This line indicates one who is emotionally open, flexible, balanced, and grounded. This person has an awareness of and respect for others. They enjoy socializing, but are not the sort to overstay their welcome.

+ **CURVED UPWARD BETWEEN THE JUPITER AND SATURN FINGER:** This suggests a nurturing, expressive person, an open communicator, probably an oversharer. They may be self-sacrificing, often to their own detriment. This person is a natural nurturer of children, pets, plants, and friends.

NOTABLE MARKINGS AT THE BEGINNING OF THE LINE

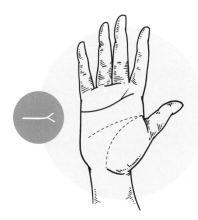

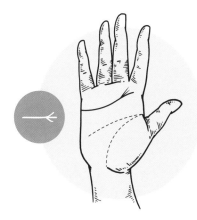

+ **FORKED:** Openness to receive love and connection.

+ **TRIDENT:** Actively attracting love and connection.

NOTABLE MARKINGS AT THE END OF THE LINE

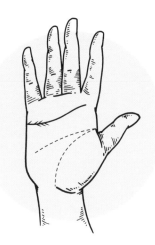

+ If the heart line ends in a tassel, it indicates someone with strong personal boundaries.

+ The absence of a tassel at the end of the heart line exhibits a lack of personal boundaries. This person may be a pushover, one who is easily taken advantage of.

OTHER MARKINGS OF NOTE

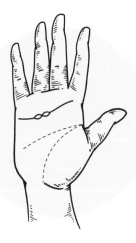

+ Islands underneath the mount of Apollo suggest that there are emotional issues relating to the need to feel validated— what one requires to be seen and heard.

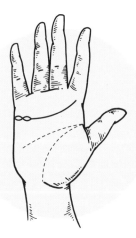

+ Islands at the end of the heart line underneath the mount of Mercury indicate challenges in communicating emotions. This can indicate trouble in discerning when or how to express the ways a person or event affected you.

Timeline

The timeline for the heart line reads horizontally across the hand, beginning with birth on the outside of the hand (thumb side), to the end of life, under the little finger. Both the heart line and head line read from right to left on the right hand or from left to right on the left hand. A break at the center of either the heart or head line can be traced to age thirty-five, since the timeline operates on our perception of time passing, not mathematics. You would then reflect on what was happening at that point in your life that could be represented by the mark.

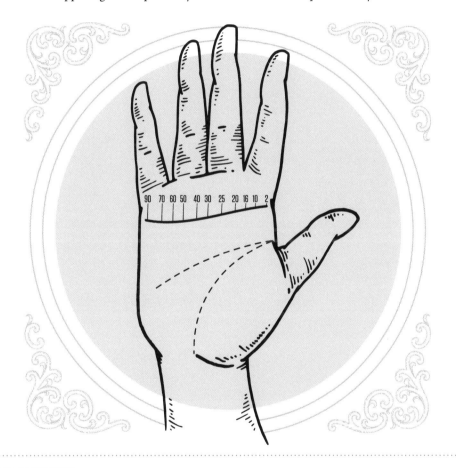

....

WORKSHEET

Label your heart line on the worksheet with a small drawing of a heart on the outside of the handprint.

+ *Write in the corresponding timeline above the line.*
+ *Observe any markings that may signify life events that affected you emotionally. Look for hairlines or vertical lines on the heart line. These may mark significant difficulties in relationships at different points in your life.*
+ *Finally, circle any line markings and notate their meaning on the sheet.*

HEAD LINE

THE HEAD LINE IS THE SECOND MAJOR LINE OF THE HAND.
Located just below the heart line, it is the line of the mind, indicating whether a person is analytical, imaginative, or somewhere in between. Splits on the head line signify an opening in perspective or a shift in thinking in conjunction with specific life events on the timeline.

OVERALL SHAPE OF THE LINE: HOW YOU THINK

+ **STRAIGHT:** Analytical. Logical. A person who doesn't love a gray area, who likes things to be clear-cut and concise—in black and white.

+ **CURVES DOWNWARD AT 15 TO 30 DEGREES:** This indicates someone who can approach circumstances analytically and intuitively. They're open to new ideas but will still form their own conclusions.

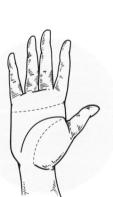

+ **CURVED DOWNWARD AT 45 DEGREES OR MORE:** This indicates extreme creativity and an abstract way of thinking. This type of head line belongs to those who don't like to deal with tedious logistics; they would prefer to envision things and create them.

+ **LONG VS. SHORT:** A long head line indicates intelligence. However, a short head line doesn't indicate a lack of it. Instead, it may indicate a person who has a difficult time focusing on tasks.

NOTABLE MARKINGS AT THE BEGINNING OF THE LINE

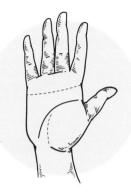 

+ **HEAD LINE BEGINS AS PART OF THE LIFE LINE:** It is common for the head line and life line to appear as one line at their start, and this initial union embodies childhood, when we are developing our identities and evolving toward independent thought. Typically, these lines split apart following puberty, between ages ten and thirteen on the timeline of the head line, when we begin to form an independent identity.

+ **HEAD LINE BEGINS SEPARATELY FROM THE LIFE LINE:** A head line beginning separately from the life line is less common than when the head and life lines begin as one. This formation can be seen on unique individuals or those who are strong-willed from youth. This could also indicate circumstances that forced a person to become more mentally self-sufficient at a young age, such as a tough home life or having to endure many physical moves.

NOTABLE MARKINGS AT THE END OF THE LINE

+ A star on the end of the head line indicates mental brilliance.

+ A triangle on the end of the head line indicates mental resilience.

+ A head line ending in Luna suggests a strong sense of intuition and imagination.

+ A break on the head line marks a time of depression or mental upheaval.

+ A split at the end of the head line marks a shift in perspective caused by life changes.

+ Chaining on the head line indicates anxiety.

The Single Transverse Palmar Crease

A single transverse palmar crease appears as one line cutting straight across the top portion of the hand, reaching to each end. These are fairly rare, and palmists view them as a fusion of the heart and head line. This line may indicate a passionate personality or someone who experiences things intensely. In such cases, this person's emotions may influence the mind for better or worse, such as leading one ambitiously toward a goal or, appositionally, decreasing motivation. If you have a single transverse palmar crease, use the heart and head line on your recessive hand to complete your reading. A double single transverse palmar crease—one on each hand— is even more rare.

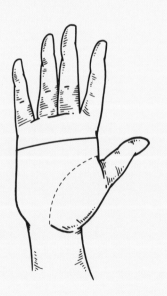

Timeline

Similar to the timeline for the heart line, the timeline for the head line reads horizontally across the hand, beginning with birth on the outside of the hand (thumb side) to the end of life, under the little finger.

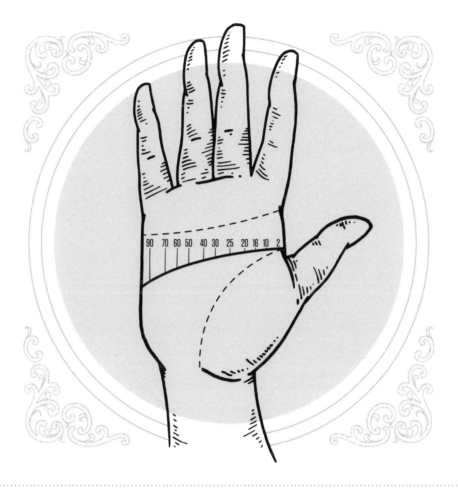

WORKSHEET

Label the head line on the worksheet with a small drawing of a stick figure face on the outside (thumb side) of the print.

+ *Write the corresponding timeline to the side of the line.*
+ *Observe any markings that may represent life events—big decisions, major changes—that challenged you mentally. Take notice of any large splits.*
+ *If markings fall on a point in the future according to the timeline, this suggests changes are on their way.*
+ *Finally, circle any notable marking and annotate its meaning on the sheet.*

LIFE LINE

THE LIFE LINE PROVIDES A NARRATIVE OF ONE'S VITALITY; IT is the life force itself. When the line fades, it may indicate difficult or unfortunate circumstances such as confusion, depression, illness, or infertility. When the life line is strong, it indicates good health and that life is satisfying and enjoyable. This line is an important player on the hand, second to the line of stability. Any markings on the life line represent critical circumstances that deeply affect our will.

The life line has its own timeline, with childhood shown on the thumb side and end of life at the bottom of the hand. If your life line does not reach the bottom of the hand, it does not mean you are going to pass at the specific age where the line ends; instead, it is a commentary on the overall state of your vitality.

OVERALL SHAPE OF THE LINE:
A MEASURE OF ENERGY LEVEL AND HEALTH

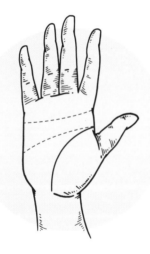 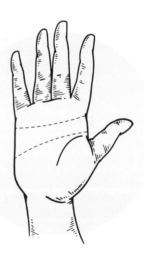

✦ **LONG VS. SHORT:** A long and deep life line isn't the promise of a long life, but a life well lived. Similarly, if the life line is short, it does not mean you will have a short life. A short life line warns that you are not embracing your life as much as you could be: you may be focusing too much on work and not enough on taking care of yourself.

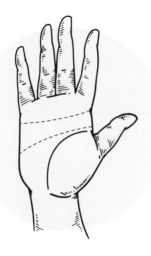

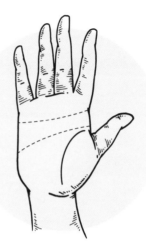

+ **LIFE LINE WITH WIDE CIRCUMFERENCE:**
A life line that swings widely around the mount of Venus indicates a warm, open, and loving person.

+ **LIFE LINE WITH NARROW CIRCUMFERENCE:**
A life line that hugs tightly around the mount of Venus suggests a reserved individual, one who is cautious about who they let into their life.

NOTABLE MARKINGS AT THE BEGINNING OF THE LINE

+ **LIFE LINE BEGINS ENTWINED WITH THE HEAD LINE:** See "Notable Markings at the Beginning of the Line" in the "Head Line" section, page 45.

+ **LIFE LINE BEGINS SEPARATELY FROM THE HEAD LINE:** See "Notable Markings at the Beginning of the Line" in the "Head Line" section, page 45.

It's your life—but only if you make it so.

—Eleanor Roosevelt, *You Learn by Living: Eleven Keys for a More Fulfilling Life*, 1960

NOTABLE MARKINGS AT THE END OF THE LINE

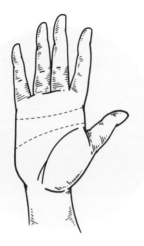 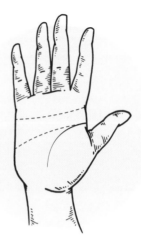

✦ **A SPLIT ON THE LINE LATER IN LIFE:** For women, this can indicate menopause. For all sexes, it can indicate a drastic life change, such as a move, retirement, or loss of a loved one.

✦ **THE LINE FADES OUT:** This suggests difficulty coping with the aging process, or possibly empty nest syndrome.

OTHER MARKINGS OF NOTE

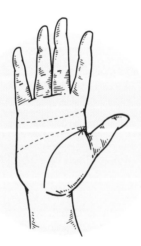 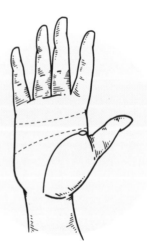

✦ A star at the start of the life line represents a traumatic birth.

✦ Islands at the beginning of the life line often represent younger siblings entering the picture, parents divorcing, or even bullying.

Timeline

The life line begins above the thumb and creates a half circle around the mount of Venus, often reaching to the middle of the bottom of the palm. The life line starts with birth on the side of the hand above the thumb, with the age of forty located directly across from where the thumb attaches to the hand, and the end of life at the top of the wrist. When there is a formation of lines at the beginning of the life line that resembles an asterisk, deemed a star in palmistry, it indicates an intense entry into the world, such as a quick or traumatic birth.

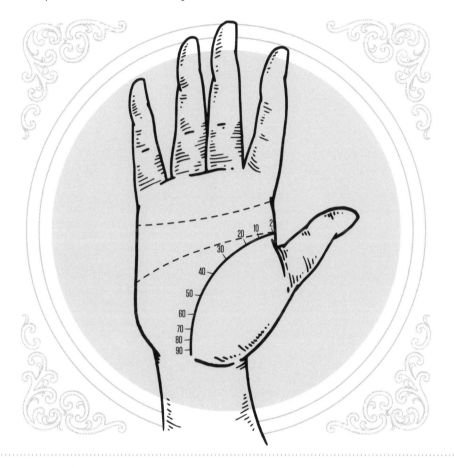

WORKSHEET

Label the life line on the worksheet with a small drawing of an ankh on the outside of the hand next to the thumb.

* *Next, write in the corresponding timeline to the side of the line.*
* *Observe any markings that may resemble life events that occurred.*
* *Note any splits or breaks, which may indicate times of depression, bad health, or feeling unsettled.*
* *Finally, circle any significant markings and note their meaning on the sheet.*

THE LINE OF STABILITY

THE LINE OF STABILITY, ALSO CALLED THE LINE OF SATURN OR the line of fate, is the definitive storyteller of a person's life journey. The line of stability starts with birth at the bottom of the hand and reads upward toward the mount of Saturn, with end of life at the top of the hand. If an island sits on the middle section of this line, this indicates a period of uncertainty in midlife related to job or financial security.

Stability in palmistry refers to career and finances, a person's mental state, or a person's physical environment. It also reflects whether you are a person who requires financial success and the acquisition of material things to feel comfortable, so much so that you will be happy working in any job that fulfills that need. In addition, it may indicate whether your emotional and mental well-being are more reliant on being true to yourself than on making a lot of money. The overall shape, markings, or end of the line can be read to reveal where a person's needs fall in this area.

OVERALL SHAPE OF THE LINE: HOW YOU COPE WITH THE UNEXPECTED

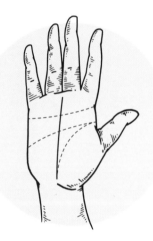 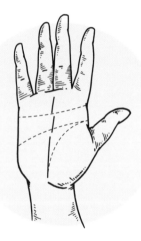

✦ **LINE IS UNBROKEN, REACHING TO TOP AND BOTTOM OF PALM:** When the line of stability is clear and stretches the entire length of the hand, it represents a powerful degree of self-confidence and trust in fate.

✦ **LINE IS BROKEN, REACHING TO TOP AND BOTTOM OF PALM:** A line of stability with breaks on either a straight or curved line indicates a person unsure about their life purpose but in the process of figuring it out. This quality of line is more common than an unbroken line, its counterpart, since it indicates the unforeseen circumstances that most of us experience.

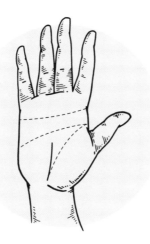

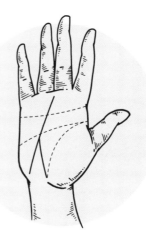

+ **SHORT LINE OF STABILITY:** This indicates a change in circumstances that affects a person's feeling of safety and security.

+ **TWO LINES OF STABILITY:** A traditional line of stability (beginning at the bottom center of the palm near the wrist and extending upward to the mount of Saturn) and an inspired line of stability (beginning at the mount of Luna and arcing upward toward the heart line) often indicates that a person is trying to make a change that results in a more authentic and motivational lifestyle.

Nothing is so painful to the human
mind as a great and sudden change.

—Mary Wollstonecraft Shelley, *Frankenstein*, 1818

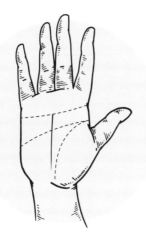

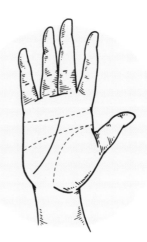

+ **BEGINNING OF LINE IS FADED:**
This indicates a lack of stability
and comfort in early life.

+ **BEGINNING OF LINE STARTS IN LUNA:**
A line of stability beginning in Luna
indicates deep creativity. Artists very
often display this line formation.

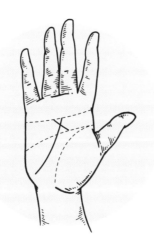

+ **BEGINNING OF LINE STARTS IN LUNA AND
INTERSECTS MYSTIC CROSS:** A mystic
cross (see page 58) is a sign possessed
by individuals who have a strong
interest in spiritual matters. A line
of stability that begins in the mount
of Luna and runs through a mystic
cross means that the person believes
themselves to be guided by destiny.

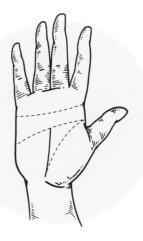

+ **LINE ENDS AT HEAD LINE:** This suggests a person who has very traditional ideas about what constitutes stability: the attainment and responsibility of family life—a day job, a home, and a car—and all that comes with it.

+ **LINE ENDS AT HEART LINE:** This marking indicates one driven by their passion to create a life based on authenticity. Often this line is seen on the palms of artists, healers, and the like.

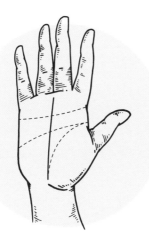

+ **LINE ENDS AT MOUNT OF APOLLO:** The promise of stability. This suggests someone who is taken care of financially, perhaps a stay-at-home mom or dad or someone with an inheritance. It may also suggest a person who is confident in their ability to provide for themselves.

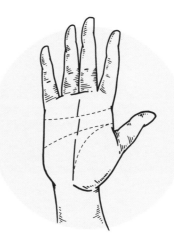

✦ **BEGINNING OF LINE HAS ISLAND:** This suggests a period of uncertainty in childhood, perhaps on someone who didn't feel safe or comfortable, either with themselves or in their surroundings, at that time in their life.

✦ **BREAKS ON THE LINE:** Breaks symbolize shifts and changes in career or lifestyle. See the timeline (opposite) to determine the age at which these events occurred or will occur.

Experience is the only thing that brings knowledge, and the longer you are on earth the more experience you are sure to get.

—L. Frank Baum, *The Wonderful Wizard of Oz*, 1900

Timeline

The timeline for the line of stability reads vertically across the hand, beginning with birth at the bottom of the hand, near the wrist, to the end of life at the top of the hand, toward the fingers.

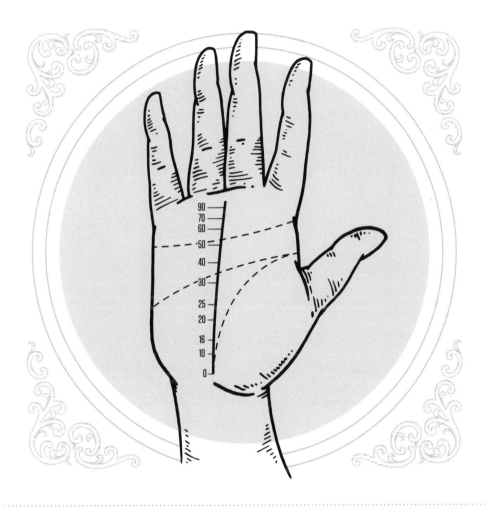

WORKSHEET

Label the line of stability on the worksheet with a small drawing of an anchor at the bottom of the line underneath your handprint.

+ *Next, write in the corresponding timeline to the side of the line.*
+ *Observe any line markings. Take notice of any splits, fades, or breaks in relationship to the timeline, since they reflect unforeseen circumstances that affected your lifestyle over the years. If the markings indicate a future event, there may be changes or opportunities on their way.*
+ *Finally, circle any notable markings related to the line and write them down on the sheet.*

MINOR LINES

IN ADDITION TO THE FOUR MAJOR LINES, OTHER LINES MAY BE found on the palm. These are called minor lines. They are listed here, from the most common to the least common.

+ **AFFECTION LINES:** Affection lines represent a person's deepest romantic relationships. They are located on the outside of the mount of Mercury, underneath the little finger, and they work on a broad timeline. The section that sits directly underneath the little finger correlates to early life, moving down the hand to later life, above the end of the heart line. Count the lines and compare that number to the number of important relationships you've had thus far. If you're currently married, look for a deep longer line. If you have had a divorce, look for a line with a split at the end.

+ **WORRY LINES:** Horizontal lines on the mount of Venus are called worry lines. A few deep lines indicate a small number of serious worries. Many deep lines can signify general anxiety. Alternately, a few light lines indicate small concerns, while many small lines mean many small concerns.

+ **LINE OF HEALTH:** The line of health, also known as the line of Mercury, runs up the hand toward the mount of Mercury, with beginning of life at the bottom of the line and end of life at the top, nearer to the mount. A solid, straight line represents exceptional health, while a scattered line indicates stress that affects general health. A line that falls somewhere between straight and scattered is a sign of unstable health or health scares.

+ **LINE OF APOLLO:** A single strong vertical line on the mount of Apollo indicates great success or being perceived as successful. A grid or multiple overlapping lines on this mount signifies a blockage—the breakthrough to success is not happening just yet.

+ **MYSTIC CROSS:** A mystic cross is an X connected between the heart and head lines. Mystic crosses signify an interest in the unseen. (If you bought this kit, chances are you have one.) Multiple mystic crosses represent strong intuitive gifts.

+ **PAST LIVES:** Horizontal lines on the outside of Luna are called travel lines. Travel lines on Luna indicate a person who has had past lives. The more lines one has, the more past lives one has lived.

+ **SPIRIT GUIDES:** Horizontal lines located on the outside of the Jupiter finger represent spirit guides—possibly angels, fairies, or people who have passed away—and may be

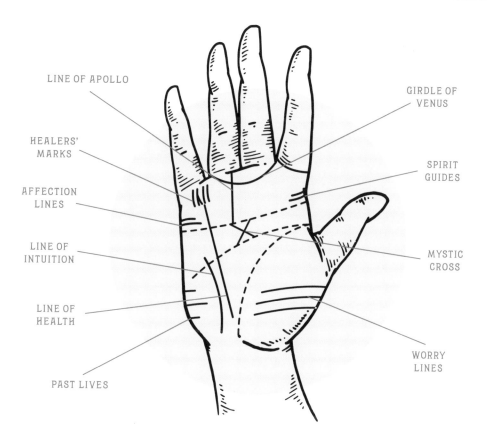

LINE OF APOLLO

HEALERS' MARKS

AFFECTION LINES

LINE OF INTUITION

LINE OF HEALTH

PAST LIVES

GIRDLE OF VENUS

SPIRIT GUIDES

MYSTIC CROSS

WORRY LINES

interpreted according to what rings true with you. A typical hand contains three of these lines. A line with a split at the end indicates an openness to making a connection to spirits. A star represents an exceptionally powerful spirit watching over you. A line that splits open suggests that you are open to the idea of spirit guides.

◆ **HEALERS' MARKS:** Four or more vertical lines on the mount of Mercury are marks of a healer. While "healer" suggests physical healing, it may also refer to a person who finds profound fulfillment when helping others or a person possessing a natural instinct to help others, even if it is only in the act of being present or holding space for others in need.

◆ **GIRDLE OF VENUS:** The girdle of Venus is an upside-down half circle placed on the mounts of Saturn and Apollo that appears to hug the corresponding fingers; it is an extension of the Venus archetype and reflects the sensuality of an individual. A deep, clear line represents assertive passion—not merely physical passion, but creative passion as well. A poorly formed girdle of Venus suggests self-doubt in these areas.

◆ **LINE OF INTUITION:** A half circle hugging the mount of Luna and facing the outer part of your palm, this rare mark indicates strong intuitive activity. People with this mark cannot ignore gut feelings and are receptive to signs from their environment.

READING THE HANDS TOGETHER

COMBINING THE INDIVIDUAL NARRATIVES HELD IN EACH OF YOUR hands into one cohesive story provides a way to track your path through life. The timeline on your dominant hand is evolving, reflecting who you are now, with clear perspective on your past as well as hints of what may lie ahead. Your recessive hand shows this same timeline, but from a more resolved viewpoint: the end of your life journey. In this way, it represents the future, but a future where you are looking back at the life you have lived.

This integrated story exposes possibilities for personal growth, healing, and the attainment of goals. If the hands appear to be exact reflections of each other, this can imply that this person may not have faced any major disruptions on their path yet. When there are difficulties or obstacles that align on both hands, the assumption is that certain lessons have been placed on a life path for a reason to be unveiled in the future.

When the hands hold major differences, it is helpful to view the dominant hand as "present you" and the recessive hand as "future you." Say you are thirty years old, and there is a break on the head line occurring at that age, according to the timeline of the line on the dominant hand. Look at this marker as a reflection of your current state of mind. This break in the line could indicate that you lost your job and are having trouble deciding what to do next.

Now compare the head line on the dominant hand with the head line on the recessive hand. If no break exists on the recessive hand, we can assume this hardship will pass. It is rare for this descriptive of a marking to appear on both hands, but if it does, whatever this marking represents is a destined event and will remain an important piece of your life journey.

HOW TO READ THE HANDS

OBSERVE YOUR TWO HANDS TOGETHER. HOLDING THEM SIDE BY side, palms up, with little fingers touching, like an open book, take note of the following:

SIMILARITIES
How to Interpret

+ Curved heart lines on both hands suggest that you were meant to care for others.

+ A deep, straight head line on both hands indicates one who is gifted and possesses an unwavering wisdom and intelligence.

+ When the life line is of the same length and unbroken on both hands, it suggests a predestined passage through life.

+ If the line of stability has the same formation on both palms, it indicates someone who has made peace with the lifestyle she leads.

DIFFERENCES
How to Interpret

+ Heart lines of a different quality—including shape, depth, and markings—on each hand speak to emotional transformation. For example, a recessive hand with a rational heart line (straight) may grow to be open and balanced in the dominant hand (curved).

+ A head line that is longer on the recessive hand than on the dominant one suggests there is potential for future learning experiences that will result in greater wisdom.

+ A life line that contains a break on the dominant hand but not on the recessive one illustrates that there will be an effective healing process.

+ The line of stability is, unsurprisingly, often the most different between the hands. It's common to see breaks, curves, and fading on the dominant hand—they represent the changes and uncertainties of the journey of life. As your life's map is written, the recessive hand presents a less chaotic, more complete representation of your time on this earth.

WORKSHEET

The worksheet is intended to be used with your dominant hand because this hand is believed to change over the course of your life. Nevertheless, printing and reading your recessive hand on a worksheet will provide more practice and can help in obtaining a clearer comprehension when comparing the two hands together.

BIBLIOGRAPHY

Association of Independent Readers and Root-workers. "Palmistry." July 3, 2018; http://readersandrootworkers.org/wiki/Category:Palmistry, accessed December 12, 2018.

Barr, Alfred H. *Picasso: Fifty Years of His Art*. New York: Arno Press/Museum of Modern Art, 1980.

Baum, Frank L. *The Wonderful Wizard of Oz*. 1900. Reprint, New York: Barnes & Noble Classics, 2005.

Bolton, Lesley. *The Everything Classical Mythology Book*. Avon, MA: Adams Media Corporation, 2002.

Cummins, Harold, and Charles Midlo. *Finger Prints, Palms, and Soles: An Introduction to Dermatoglyphics*. 1943. Reprint, South Berlin, MA: Research Publishing Company, 1976.

Goldberg, Ellen, and Dorian Bergen. *The Art and Science of Hand Reading: Classical Methods for Self-Discovery Through Palmistry*. Rochester, VT: Destiny Books, 2016.

Hamilton, Edith. *Mythology: Timeless Tales of Gods and Heroes*. 1942. Reprint, New York: Black Dog & Leventhal Publishers, 2017.

Jones, Christopher. "Captain Casimir D'Arpentigny—Founding Father of Chirognomy." Johnny Fincham Palmistry; http://www.johnnyfincham.com/history/darpentigny.htm, accessed December 5, 2018.

Look and Learn. "The Incredible Count Cheiro Predicted the Abdication." Look and Learn History Picture Library. January 23, 2014; https://www.lookandlearn.com/blog/29898/the-incredible-count-cheiro-predicted-the-abdication/, accessed December 8, 2018.

Mensvoort, Martijn van. "Simian Line Research—The Notorious Single Palmar Crease." Hand Research; http://simianline.handresearch.com/, accessed December 8, 2018.

Oseid, Kelsey. *What We See in the Stars: An Illustrated Tour of the Night Sky*. Berkeley, CA: Ten Speed Press, 2017.

Phillpotts, Eden. *A Shadow Passes*. 1918. Reprint, London: Forgotten Books, 2018.

Poppele, Jonathan. *Night Sky*. Cambridge, MN: Adventure Publications, 2009.

Price, Simon, and Emily Kearns. *The Oxford Dictionary of Classical Myth and Religion*. Oxford: Oxford University Press, 2003.

Rilke, Rainer Maria. *Letters to a Young Poet*, translated by M. D. Herter Norton. 1934. Reprint, New York: W.W. Norton, 1993.

Roosevelt, Eleanor. *You Learn by Living: Eleven Keys for a More Fulfilling Life*. 1960. Reprint, New York: Harper Perennial, 2016.

Rumi, Jalal al-Din. "The Guest House." In *The Essential Rumi*, translated by Coleman Barks. 1995. Reprint, New York: HarperOne, 2004.

Saint-Exupéry, Antoine de. *The Little Prince*. 1943. Reprint, San Diego: Harcourt, 2000.

Shakespeare, William, and George Richard Hibbard. *Hamlet*. 1603. Reprint, Oxford, UK: Oxford University Press, 2008.

Shelley, Mary Wollstonecraft. *Frankenstein*. 1818. Reprint, New York: W. W. Norton & Company, 2012.

Shesso, Renna. *A Magical Tour of the Night Sky: Use the Planets and Stars for Personal and Sacred Discovery*. San Francisco: Weiser, 2011.

Thoreau, Henry David. *Walden, or, Life in the Woods*. 1854. Reprint, New York: Vintage, 2014.

Unger, Richard. *Lifeprints: Deciphering Your Life Purpose from Your Fingerprints*. Berkeley, CA: Crossing Press, 2007.

ABOUT THE AUTHOR

HELENE SAUCEDO is a hand analyst who provides private readings out of her vintage camper and travels, practicing her craft, lecturing, and reading at shops and events such as Bonnaroo, Dirty South Yoga Festival, and the McKittrick Hotel. She also has a background in design and art direction, with more than ten years' experience working with brands such as Turner Broadcasting, Cartoon Network Latin America, Steve Madden, and Macmillan Publishers. She lives in Atlanta, Georgia.

HANDFULOFSTARSREADINGS.COM

Instagram: @handfulofstars_readings

Facebook: @HandfulofStarsReadings

The universe is full of
magical things, patiently
waiting for our wits to
grow sharper.

—Eden Phillpotts, *A Shadow Passes*, 1918

NAME . . . . DATE . . . . AGE . . . .

HAND FLEXIBILITY . . . .

THUMB SIZE . . . .

LOGIC VS. WILL . . . .

THUMB ANGLE . . . .

MOUNTS	ELEMENTAL SHAPE
♃ **JUPITER** AMBITION · CONFIDENCE A LEADER	▽ **EARTH** PRACTICAL · GROUNDED REALISTIC
♄ **SATURN** DISCIPLINE · LIFE BALANCE WORK ETHIC	△ **FIRE** RESTLESS · ANXIOUS WARM
☉ **APOLLO (SUN)** CREATIVE · IMAGINATIVE OPEN-MINDED	△ **AIR** INTELLECTUAL · CURIOUS ADAPTABLE
☿ **MERCURY** COMMUNICATION · PROBLEM SOLVING A SPEAKER	▽ **WATER** SENSITIVE · EMPATHIC EMOTIONAL
♀ **VENUS** LOVE · BEAUTY PLEASURE	
☽ **LUNA (MOON)** INTUITION · SPIRITUALITY A DREAMER	
♂ **MARS** BRAVE · RESILIENT A WARRIOR	

MOUNT MARKINGS

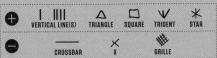

⊕ | |||| VERTICAL LINE(S) △ TRIANGLE ▢ SQUARE ⋁ TRIDENT ✳ STAR
⊖ — CROSSBAR ✕ X ▦ GRILLE

KEY FOR LINES

♡ HEART 🦉 HEAD ♀ LIFE ⚓ STABILITY

LINE MARKINGS

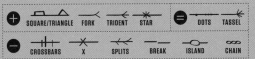

⊕ SQUARE/TRIANGLE FORK TRIDENT STAR ⊜ DOTS TASSEL
⊖ CROSSBARS X SPLITS BREAK ISLAND CHAIN

HAND FLEXIBILITY ....

THUMB SIZE ....

LOGIC VS. WILL ....

THUMB ANGLE ....

MOUNTS

JUPITER
AMBITION · CONFIDENCE
A LEADER

SATURN
DISCIPLINE · LIFE BALANCE
WORK ETHIC

APOLLO (SUN)
CREATIVE · IMAGINATIVE
OPEN-MINDED

MERCURY
COMMUNICATION · PROBLEM SOLVING
A SPEAKER

VENUS
LOVE · BEAUTY
PLEASURE

LUNA (MOON)
INTUITION · SPIRITUALITY
A DREAMER

MARS
BRAVE · RESILIENT
A WARRIOR

ELEMENTAL SHAPE

▽

EARTH
PRACTICAL · GROUNDED
REALISTIC

△

FIRE
RESTLESS · ANXIOUS
WARM

AIR
INTELLECTUAL · CURIOUS
ADAPTABLE

▽

WATER
SENSITIVE · EMPATHIC
EMOTIONAL

MOUNT MARKINGS

⊕	VERTICAL LINE(S)	TRIANGLE	SQUARE	TRIDENT	STAR
⊖	CROSSBAR	X	GRILLE		

KEY FOR LINES

HEART	HEAD	LIFE	STABILITY

LINE MARKINGS

⊕	SQUARE/TRIANGLE	FORK	TRIDENT	STAR	⊜	DOTS	TASSEL
⊖	CROSSBARS	X	SPLITS	BREAK	ISLAND	CHAIN	

Handful of Stars ©

NAME .... DATE .... AGE ....

HAND FLEXIBILITY ....

THUMB SIZE ....

LOGIC VS. WILL ....

THUMB ANGLE ....

MOUNTS

♃ JUPITER
AMBITION · CONFIDENCE
A LEADER

♄ SATURN
DISCIPLINE · LIFE BALANCE
WORK ETHIC

☉ APOLLO (SUN)
CREATIVE · IMAGINATIVE
OPEN-MINDED

☿ MERCURY
COMMUNICATION · PROBLEM SOLVING
A SPEAKER

♀ VENUS
LOVE · BEAUTY
PLEASURE

☽ LUNA (MOON)
INTUITION · SPIRITUALITY
A DREAMER

♂ MARS
BRAVE · RESILIENT
A WARRIOR

ELEMENTAL SHAPE

▽
EARTH
PRACTICAL · GROUNDED
REALISTIC

△
FIRE
RESTLESS · ANXIOUS
WARM

△
AIR
INTELLECTUAL · CURIOUS
ADAPTABLE

▽
WATER
SENSITIVE · EMPATHIC
EMOTIONAL

MOUNT MARKINGS

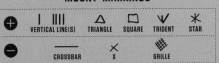

⊕ | |||| VERTICAL LINE(S)   △ TRIANGLE   ▢ SQUARE   ∨ TRIDENT   ✳ STAR

⊖ CROSSBAR   ✕ X   ▦ GRILLE

KEY FOR LINES

♡ HEART   HEAD   LIFE   ⚓ STABILITY

LINE MARKINGS

⊕ SQUARE/TRIANGLE   FORK   TRIDENT   STAR   ⊖ DOTS   TASSEL

⊖ CROSSBARS   X   SPLITS   BREAK   ISLAND   CHAIN

NAME .... DATE .... AGE ....

HAND FLEXIBILITY ....

THUMB SIZE ....

LOGIC VS. WILL ....

THUMB ANGLE ....

MOUNTS

♃
JUPITER
AMBITION · CONFIDENCE
A LEADER

♄
SATURN
DISCIPLINE · LIFE BALANCE
WORK ETHIC

☉
APOLLO (SUN)
CREATIVE · IMAGINATIVE
OPEN-MINDED

☿
MERCURY
COMMUNICATION · PROBLEM SOLVING
A SPEAKER

♀
VENUS
LOVE · BEAUTY
PLEASURE

☽
LUNA (MOON)
INTUITION · SPIRITUALITY
A DREAMER

♂
MARS
BRAVE · RESILIENT
A WARRIOR

ELEMENTAL SHAPE

▽
EARTH
PRACTICAL · GROUNDED
REALISTIC

▢

△
FIRE
RESTLESS · ANXIOUS
WARM

▢

△̶
AIR
INTELLECTUAL · CURIOUS
ADAPTABLE

▢

▽
WATER
SENSITIVE · EMPATHIC
EMOTIONAL

▢

MOUNT MARKINGS

⊕ | VERTICAL LINE(S) | △ TRIANGLE | ▢ SQUARE | ⅄ TRIDENT | ✳ STAR

⊖ ― CROSSBAR | ✕ X | ▦ GRILLE

KEY FOR LINES

♡ HEART | ⊗ HEAD | ☥ LIFE | ⚓ STABILITY

LINE MARKINGS

⊕ SQUARE/TRIANGLE | FORK | TRIDENT | STAR | ⊜ DOTS | TASSEL

⊖ CROSSBARS | X | SPLITS | BREAK | ISLAND | CHAIN

NAME .... DATE .... AGE ....

HAND FLEXIBILITY ....

THUMB SIZE ....

LOGIC VS. WILL ....

THUMB ANGLE ....

MOUNTS

♃ JUPITER
AMBITION · CONFIDENCE
A LEADER

♄ SATURN
DISCIPLINE · LIFE BALANCE
WORK ETHIC

☉ APOLLO (SUN)
CREATIVE · IMAGINATIVE
OPEN-MINDED

☿ MERCURY
COMMUNICATION · PROBLEM SOLVING
A SPEAKER

♀ VENUS
LOVE · BEAUTY
PLEASURE

☽ LUNA (MOON)
INTUITION · SPIRITUALITY
A DREAMER

♂ MARS
BRAVE · RESILIENT
A WARRIOR

ELEMENTAL SHAPE

▽

EARTH
PRACTICAL · GROUNDED
REALISTIC

FIRE
RESTLESS · ANXIOUS
WARM

AIR
INTELLECTUAL · CURIOUS
ADAPTABLE

WATER
SENSITIVE · EMPATHIC
EMOTIONAL

MOUNT MARKINGS

⊕ | |||| VERTICAL LINE(S) △ TRIANGLE ▢ SQUARE ⩔ TRIDENT ✳ STAR

⊖ — CROSSBAR ✕ X ▦ GRILLE

KEY FOR LINES

♡ HEART   HEAD   LIFE   ⚓ STABILITY

LINE MARKINGS

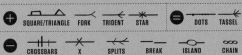

⊕ SQUARE/TRIANGLE FORK TRIDENT STAR ⊜ DOTS TASSEL

⊖ CROSSBARS X SPLITS BREAK ISLAND CHAIN

NAME .... DATE .... AGE ....

HAND FLEXIBILITY ....

THUMB SIZE ....

LOGIC VS. WILL ....

THUMB ANGLE ....

MOUNTS

JUPITER
AMBITION · CONFIDENCE
A LEADER

♄
SATURN
DISCIPLINE · LIFE BALANCE
WORK ETHIC

☉
APOLLO (SUN)
CREATIVE · IMAGINATIVE
OPEN-MINDED

☿
MERCURY
COMMUNICATION · PROBLEM SOLVING
A SPEAKER

♀
VENUS
LOVE · BEAUTY
PLEASURE

☾
LUNA (MOON)
INTUITION · SPIRITUALITY
A DREAMER

♂
MARS
BRAVE · RESILIENT
A WARRIOR

ELEMENTAL SHAPE

▽
EARTH
PRACTICAL · GROUNDED
REALISTIC

△
FIRE
RESTLESS · ANXIOUS
WARM

△
AIR
INTELLECTUAL · CURIOUS
ADAPTABLE

▽
WATER
SENSITIVE · EMPATHIC
EMOTIONAL

MOUNT MARKINGS

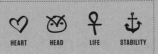

KEY FOR LINES

HEART   HEAD   LIFE   STABILITY

LINE MARKINGS

NAME .... **DATE** .... **AGE** ....

HAND FLEXIBILITY ....

THUMB SIZE ....

LOGIC VS. WILL ....

THUMB ANGLE ....

MOUNTS

♃ JUPITER
AMBITION · CONFIDENCE
A LEADER

♄ SATURN
DISCIPLINE · LIFE BALANCE
WORK ETHIC

☉ APOLLO (SUN)
CREATIVE · IMAGINATIVE
OPEN-MINDED

☿ MERCURY
COMMUNICATION · PROBLEM SOLVING
A SPEAKER

♀ VENUS
LOVE · BEAUTY
PLEASURE

☽ LUNA (MOON)
INTUITION · SPIRITUALITY
A DREAMER

♂ MARS
BRAVE · RESILIENT
A WARRIOR

ELEMENTAL SHAPE

▽ EARTH
PRACTICAL · GROUNDED
REALISTIC

△ FIRE
RESTLESS · ANXIOUS
WARM

△ AIR
INTELLECTUAL · CURIOUS
ADAPTABLE

▽ WATER
SENSITIVE · EMPATHIC
EMOTIONAL

MOUNT MARKINGS

⊕ | VERTICAL LINE(S) | TRIANGLE | SQUARE | TRIDENT | STAR
⊖ | CROSSBAR | X | GRILLE

KEY FOR LINES

HEART · HEAD · LIFE · STABILITY

LINE MARKINGS

⊕ SQUARE/TRIANGLE | FORK | TRIDENT | STAR | ═ DOTS | TASSEL
⊖ CROSSBARS | X | SPLITS | BREAK | ISLAND | CHAIN

NAME .... DATE .... AGE ....

HAND FLEXIBILITY ....

THUMB SIZE ....

LOGIC VS. WILL ....

THUMB ANGLE ....

MOUNTS

♃
JUPITER
AMBITION · CONFIDENCE
A LEADER

♄
SATURN
DISCIPLINE · LIFE BALANCE
WORK ETHIC

☉
APOLLO (SUN)
CREATIVE · IMAGINATIVE
OPEN-MINDED

☿
MERCURY
COMMUNICATION · PROBLEM SOLVING
A SPEAKER

♀
VENUS
LOVE · BEAUTY
PLEASURE

☽
LUNA (MOON)
INTUITION · SPIRITUALITY
A DREAMER

♂
MARS
BRAVE · RESILIENT
A WARRIOR

ELEMENTAL SHAPE

▽
EARTH
PRACTICAL · GROUNDED
REALISTIC

△
FIRE
RESTLESS · ANXIOUS
WARM

△ (with line)
AIR
INTELLECTUAL · CURIOUS
ADAPTABLE

▽ (with line)
WATER
SENSITIVE · EMPATHIC
EMOTIONAL